The Muslimah Sex Manual

A Halal Guide to Mind Blowing Sex

Contents:

Acknowledgements

This book could not have been written without the encouragement of those around me. I would like to thank Zainab bint Younus who blogs at The Salafi Feminist for reading and reviewing a manuscript of this book. I would also like to thank Nabeel Azeez who blogs at Becoming the Alpha Muslim for his help in marketing this book.

There are several other people whose help was invaluable but would prefer to stay anonymous. They have my heartfelt thanks and appreciation.

Ready?

I'll take you down this delightful rabbit hole of pleasure. Let me warn you, this is not for the faint of heart. I'm going to talk about things that you would never bring up in conversation. I will teach you how to make your husband look at you with unbridled lust. You will find your husband transformed into a man who can't keep his hands off of you and brims with jealousy when other men so much as glance at you.

If you're unprepared for that, put this book away.

If not, let's begin.

Introduction

Two years ago, I was congratulating a young Muslimah on her engagement. She had grown up in my community and I had known her since before she could talk. I had seen her blossom from a waddling toddler into a confident and intelligent young woman. She began looking for a husband in her last year of college, wanting to get married before starting medical school. After multiple dead-ends, she had finally found a man who met all her criteria for marriage. Everything about this guy was perfect. He was religious, good looking, volunteered at the masjid, had a stable job, was known for his kindness to youngsters at the masjid, and was loved by the elders like he was their own nephew. It was a perfect match. She was thrilled about starting married life and you could see the happiness emanating from her as everyone gave her their best wishes.

A few months later, I ran into her at a dinner party and asked how marriage life was suiting her. She simply said it was "Fine", but I could tell something was wrong.

After some cajoling, she shamefully admitted the truth. Her sex life was horrible. In fact, it was fast becoming non-existent. She had been a model Muslimah her entire life. Before marriage, she had never so much as held a non-mahram's hand, let alone become physically intimate with one. She had eagerly looked forward to marriage as a chance to finally indulge in all the physical intimacy she had postponed for the sake of Allah.

But it wasn't working.

Coming from the medical field, she knew all the relevant biology. She could draw and label all the parts of male and female anatomy. She had taken fiqh classes and knew the legal rulings of menstruation and intercourse.

But she didn't know *sex*.

Oh, she knew the mechanics. Insert penis into vagina. Climax. Withdraw. But she didn't know how to make her husband yearn for her in bed. She didn't know what he liked. She didn't even know what *she* liked! They had begun eagerly but after a few weeks, realized that neither of them was truly enjoying having sex with each other.

As I talked more to her, I found out that she had never orgasmed during sex. Not once in the six months she'd been married. She shyly confessed to me that she had been masturbating since high school and was afraid that she had ruined her body doing it. She thought maybe she had conditioned herself to only enjoy self-pleasure.

She couldn't look me in the eyes as she asked if that was the reason why she couldn't orgasm with her husband.

And so began my impromptu sex skills workshop. I threw at her all the information I'd gathered over years of marriage. Things I'd learned from experience, tidbits I'd gleaned from friends, tips I'd picked up from magazine articles. One thing here, two things there. All those bits had accumulated into a very healthy and robust sex life between my husband and I. I gave her everything, fervently hoping that it would help her in her marital life.

A month later, I saw her again. This time she had a gigantic smile on her face. "Please, write this down and share it with other Muslim girls. No one teaches this. We're thrown into marriage and only know the fiqh and the biology."

I wrote down everything I told her on a Word document and emailed it to her. She shared it with her friends who were newly married. They shared it with their friends. Before long, word trickled back to me that people were asking me to write a book on the subject.

So here it is.

Who is this book for?

Perhaps you're getting married soon and are apprehensive about sex. Maybe you've been married for a few years and your bedroom life has become dull. Or maybe you're already in a raunchy, fulfilling sexual relationship with your husband and are looking for something extra to spice it up.

This book is for all of you.

As a necessary disclaimer, this book is **only** for people who intend to use the information in the book for their marriage. I free myself from anyone who uses this book to help them have premarital or extramarital sex. This book is written by a religious, practicing Muslim for other religious, practicing Muslims. I do not agree with the liberal mentality that "sex is just an action" and that consent is the only thing which determines right or wrong. Right and wrong are determined by the Qur'an and Sunnah and any action which contravenes Divine scripture is, by definition, wrong. My book is written to enhance marital joy and pleasure. It is written to make fulfilling marriages and to increase happiness between a husband and his wife. If you use it for something other than that, I leave your punishment to Allah.

I do not claim to be a scholar and refrain from passing any fatawa in this book. However, this book is written for orthodox, practicing Muslims, and so I have purposefully ignored things which are considered unanimously haram. You will not find instructions on how to enjoy anal sex or suggestions to watch pornography with your husband.

The fiqh methodology of this book does not exclusively follow any specific madhab. Where I deemed necessary, I have inserted scholarly rulings from scholars I trust. I have not done this for every single issue in order to avoid making this a fiqh manual. If you are skeptical about the permissibility of anything in this book, you should consult a scholar you trust.

Myths

Before I begin the actual book, here are five of the most common myths about Muslims and sex. Beat these myths out of your head before beginning.

Myth 1: A pure Muslim can't be dirty in bed

I don't know who started this myth but it is flat out wrong. We have halal and we have haram. Any sexual encounters outside of marriage is haram. Everything inside marriage is halal (other than a tiny number of things which I will mention in the book). You can be pure as snow and still be very dirty in bed. What is amusing (in a sad way) is that many younger Muslims think that the practicing, masjid going, hijab/niqab wearing sisters have dull sex lives and never venture outside of the vanilla. Not true! I have a theory that Muslims are actually kinkier than non-Muslims because we bottle up all that sexual energy and provide only one outlet, that of marriage. Whatever the reason though, I can assure you that some of the same Muslim men and women giving halaqahs and khutbahs and volunteering at the masjid are having very raunchy sex behind closed doors. Being a pure Muslim doesn't mean you don't enjoy sex. It means doing all of that only in marriage and not advertising your bedroom secrets to everyone. In the privacy of your bedroom and between you and your spouse, you can enjoy a very, very rollicking sex life.

The famous Andalusian scholar, Ibn Hazm, wrote this:

> But I have observed that many men err gravely as to the true meaning of the word "righteousness." Its correct interpretation is as follows. The "righteous" woman is one who, when duly restrained, restrains herself; when temptations are kept out of her way, she keeps herself under control. The "wicked" woman on the other hand is one who, when duly restrained, does not restrain herself, and when barred from all facilities for committing licence, nevertheless herself contrives by some ruse or other to discover the means of behaving badly. The "righteous" man is he who has no traffic with adulterers, and does not expose himself to sights exciting the passions; who does not raise his eyes to look

upon ravishing shapes and forms. The "wicked" man however is he who consorts with depraved people, who allows his gaze to wander freely and stares avidly at beautiful faces, who seeks out harmful spectacles and delights in deadly privacies. The "righteous" man and the "righteous" woman are like a fire that lies hidden within the ashes, and does not burn any who is within range of it unless it be stirred into flame.

Having that fire burn within you isn't a sign that you're a bad person. Lacking that fire isn't a sign of righteousness. Righteousness is deciding to only stir that fire into a flame within the bounds of marriage.

Myth 2: The only way for a Muslim to learn how to be great in bed is by doing haram things before marriage

This is another myth that many Muslims have fallen for. A Muslim girl once told me that she wanted to marry a non-practicing Muslim man or a convert because he's likely done zina and thus would be better in bed! This is completely false and it's terrible that people think like this! I had zero intimate relations before marriage. The first time I kissed a man, it was my husband. My husband was the same. I am the only woman he has ever been physically intimate with and I have no complaints about him in the bedroom. I have non-Muslim friends who were sexually active in college and still came to me for advice because they didn't know how to have fun in bed. There is no correlation between having sex before marriage and being great in bed. Thinking that doing haram is going to make your halal relationship better is faulty reasoning. The opposite is true. Saving the physical intimacy of sex for only your husband strengthens your bond. This is a man who has announced his relationship to you in public, taken responsibility for shouldering your expenses, and is willing to step up to the plate and be a true father and husband. *That* man will please you in bed. Not a man who added notches to his bedpost in order to brag to his friends.

Myth 3: Porn is a great educational tool

Statistically, this is a bigger problem for men than women. There's still a sizeable number of Muslim women who turn to pornography though. Let me tell you in very simple English: Porn is a lie. Real sex is not like pornography. Porn is recorded in order to be entertaining *to the viewer.* Positions which *look* the best are chosen, not ones which are necessarily the most enojyable. It's not the same as real sex. Real sex is sweaty. Real sex has inevitable farts and queefs. Real sex can get smelly. Real sex consists of men and women with imperfect bodies and a need for foreplay. Real sex comes with emotions. Porn is acting. Women are sexual objects in porn, a vessel for male enjoyment. Women fake their moans, they contort their facial expressions, they pretend to enjoy the most uncomfortable positions. The man supposedly makes them orgasm every single time with just vaginal penetration. And talk about unattainable standards! For men *and* women (but more for women). Even porn stars don't look like porn stars. Before a shoot, they have professional makeup artists work on their face. Most have had plastic surgery. None are overweight. The men are all muscular with gigantic penises. They ejaculate more loads than is humanly possible. Don't get fooled into thinking this is real or that your sex life should resemble a porn video. Research shows that people who watch porn feel worse about the way they look as well as the way their partner looks. In short, porn is one of the worst ways to learn about sex.

Myth 4: Women's magazines and books written by PhDs are excellent sources of sexual education

Many women stack up on these books before marriage. But guess what? Getting a PhD is simply a matter of spending time in a lab or library. That's not sex. You might learn some interesting psychology or physiology, but that's not learning sex. You're making the same mistake the Muslim girl I mentioned did—thinking that knowing the biology, anatomy, and fiqh of sex means you actually *know* sex. Those books might make for interesting reading, but they're not a sex manual. This book is about *how* to have sex. The nuts and bolts of making your husband thirst for you in bed. It is not an academic publication about the physiology of an orgasm. Knowing how an orgasm occurs in the body is not going to help you achieve an orgasm yourself.

Put another way, who can best train an athlete for the Olympics? A scientist who's studied muscle development for years in a lab? Or a coach who's a former athlete and has been involved in the sport for decades?

Myth 5: Religious men lose respect for wives who are dirty in bed

Men *love* it when their wives are dirty in bed. Why would a man *not* want his wife to be great in the bedroom? Many Muslim guys worry about the opposite problem—that their wife *won't* want to be adventurous in bed. Guys want their wife to be fun in the bedroom. It doesn't bother them at all. What does bother many men is when they think their wife has done all of this with other guys. Especially pious Muslim men who've been chaste before marriage, it really messes with their mind when they think you've been unchaste and hid it from them. So if your husband is wondering where you learned all this, show him this book and tell him exactly where you learned it! Every man's dream wife is modest in public and immodest with him in the bedroom. Make that dream come true!

The Basics

Anatomy

I know I said this wasn't a book about biology but it *is* important to know some basic facts about what's going on down there. I've kept this section as short as possible, if you want to know more biology, there are plenty of textbooks with that information. If you're already familiar with the anatomy, you can skip this section as it can be a bit dry.

Female anatomy

A lot of people, even women, refer to the entire female sexual anatomy as "vagina". This isn't accurate. What most people call the "vagina" is actually the vulva. This is the outer part of your genitalia. The *mons pubis* or pubic mound is the fatty tissue over your pubic bone. This fatty tissue serves an important function of acting as a protective cushion during sex. It divides into two folds of skin called the labia majora. Some women refer to this as their "outer vaginal lips". During sex (or arousal), the labia majora fills with blood and gets bigger. It's also an erogenous zone, and the feeling you get when touching it is similar to the feeling your husband gets when you touch his scrotum. If you push the labia majora apart, you'll see a thinner set of lips called the labia minora, or as some women call it, "inner vaginal lips". They join together at the top and form a "hood" over the clitoris. The clitoral hood is the female equivalent of a man's foreskin.

The clitoris is a small little bit of tissue which is covered by this hood. It serves only one purpose—sexual pleasure. For those who think that women shouldn't enjoy sex, this is a sign from Allah. Men do not have any organ solely dedicated to sexual pleasure. The same penis they use for sex is also used for urination. For women though, the clitoris serves no purpose other than sexual pleasure. There are over eight *thousand* sensory nerve endings in an area the size of a pea.

Finally, the perineum is the area between your anus and your vulva. It too is an erogenous zone and stimulating it can feel pleasurable. The perineum is stretched during childbirth and can often tear, especially if it's your first child.

And that's just the outside bit of your anatomy!

"Vagina" is the main word we associate with female genitalia. The vagina is actually the opening/canal that goes from your vulva all the way internally to a structure called the cervix. The average depth of a vagina is 3-5 inches when unaroused and 5-8 inches deep when aroused. In terms of pleasure, the first few inches are the most sensitive. Depending on your husband's length and your depth, as well as the position you two have chosen, you may find the head of his penis hitting your cervix. For some women, this can be painful while for others, it can be pleasurable.

Male anatomy

Men are much more simple down there. You only really need to know two things: he has a penis and he has testicles.

Testicle (aka balls) are the male equivalent of your ovaries. Size can vary quite widely. Anything from grape sized testicles to egg sized testicles is normal. If your husband has pea sized testicles and is very muscular, there's a high chance his muscle mass is due to anabolic steroids. The main thing to remember about testicles is that they are *very* tender. This is not a place you should be rough. A sharp tap on a man's testicle can momentarily cripple him. Keep that in mind when you're having sex. Another thing to know is that there is no relation between size of his testicles and the amount of semen he produces. A teaspoon amount of semen is about normal for most men. Pornographic actors take supplements to increase the amount they ejaculate for filming (or, through creative camera angles, use corn syrup to give the illusion that they are ejaculating). Don't go expecting buckets of ejaculation from your husband. That's a porn fantasy as well.

The other thing down there is his penis. Unlike in a woman's genitals where there is a distinct sexual organ (the clitoris) and a place to urinate (the urethra), men have only one thing. The same place where urine exits is where semen comes out of.

I'm sure you're wondering about size. How does your husband stack up against others? Here's the data: The average length of an erect penis is between 4.5 and 5.75 inches. I did not make a typo. The mean length of an erect penis is 5.17 inches with a standard deviation of 0.65 inches. Look it up. British Journal of Urology did the largest, most systematic review on the subject in 2015. Didn't I tell you before that porn was not educational? Women who watch porn or read a lot of erotica can end up thinking that the average penis is 7 inches and that anything less than that is small. Less than 7% of men have a penis 7 inches or longer. The 8 inch penises popular in porn make up less than half of one percentage of all men. Odds are, your husband's penis is between 4 and 6 inches. He's not abnormal, that's a normal size for a penis. Another thing about penises is that they can be flaccid or erect. There's no relation between penis size when flaccid and when erect. Some men go from a 4 inch penis when flaccid to a 5 inch penis when erect. Others go from a 1.5 inch penis when flaccid to a 7 inch penis when flaccid. No relationship at all.

More importantly, most women who are unsatisfied in the bedroom are not unsatisfied because of their partner's penis size. Satisfaction in bed isn't related to his penis size (unless it is extremely small or extremely large). Whether your husband has a 4 inch penis or a 7 inch penis, he can still satisfy you in bed. Don't get disheartened if he's on the smaller size, he might be a better lover than a man who's much better endowed. On the flipside, don't be surprised if you find that you're not satisfied in bed despite having a husband who is well endowed. As you'll discover by reading this book, there's a lot more to enjoying your sex life than your husband's penis size.

Body image

If I were to randomly guess how you feel about your body, I would probably be accurate in guessing that you're worried about it. Maybe you feel a little bit overweight or maybe you feel a lot overweight. Maybe you feel like you're too flabby or not toned enough. Maybe you're ashamed of stretch marks or are worried about cellulite. Maybe you have scars on your body that bother you. Many women feel insecure about their body no matter how they actually look. I can speak forever on body image and unrealistic beauty standards but this isn't a book about that! I know, without even knowing you, that you're afraid your husband will not be pleased with your body because you're flabby/have stretch marks/have cellulite/acne/something else.

Get that out of your head!

Feeling insecure is one of the greatest ways to damage your performance in bed. When you feel insecure, you're less likely to let loose and have fun. I can't undo billions of dollars of advertising and social pressure in one page in order to make you feel secure about your body. I will say this however:

Men want to have sex.

Men enjoy sex.

Men enjoy girls who are dirty in bed.

Your husband is a man and therefore, he wants to have sex with you. He chose to marry you. He knew that he was signing on to have sex with you when he made that choice. You might have stretch marks and acne and cellulite but guess what? It doesn't matter. All women do. The sexiest thing you can do is be confident in yourself. Take ownership of your body and have fun. Your husband wants to see you naked, I guarantee it. Insha'Allah you married for piety and therefore, you will be the only woman in his life. He has no choice but to enjoy you!

Genital hygiene

Genital hygiene is a crucial part of a healthy sex life. If everything down there is smelly and hairy, the idea of sex becomes repulsive. There's a wisdom behind pubic hair removal being an obligatory part of Islam. Everything is nicer in bed when you have no hair down there. There's less odor, it looks nicer and your husband is more likely to go down on you!

At this point in your life, you probably have a routine to keep yourself bald down there. If not, here's a quick guide to hair removal.

Shaving

In order to do this most effectively, start with a good blade. Buy a good quality razor and good quality blades to go with it. Don't be stingy! The cheaper the blade and the longer you go before changing it, the greater the chance of razor burn or ingrown hairs. Not fun and not sexy.

Start by letting your skin soak for a while in warm water (i.e. take a warm shower or bath). Exfoliate your skin by using a loofah. You don't have to go crazy but firmly rub the loofah as you shower to exfoliate the skin. Some women use shaving cream to help soften the hair and skin before shaving. If you want to go natural, you can use baby oil instead of shaving cream.

When you start actually shaving, pull the skin tight so you're working with a smooth, firm surface. Shave with the grain using as few strokes as possible. Once you're done shaving with the grain, go over the same area but against the grain this time. Once you're out of the shower, blot yourself dry and apply some antiseptic to close the pores and kill bacteria. A neat trick I learned is to use odorless deodorant on your pubic area afterwards to prevent razor burn or ingrown hairs. There are also various products you can buy to prevent razor burns or ingrown hair. Every woman is different so do what works best for you!

Other options are to do home waxing, sugaring, or use an epilator. What is *not* an option, however, is to go to a salon and get a bikini wax. Exposing your awrah is not allowed without a medical necessity and this does not fall under that category.[i]

Smell

People sweat. That's just a reality. It just so happens that in between your legs is a place where sweat likes to gather. This can sometimes leads to an unpleasant odor. There's no way to completely eliminate the smell but you can take steps to minimize it. Most obviously, you should be taking a shower every day. General body hygiene goes a long way in taking care of odors. After that, you can combat smell by using scents. After you shower in the morning, take an itr stick and lightly dab a drop where your legs join your torso. Use itr not perfume. The oil base of the itr make it stay there and the heat from your legs will gradually release the smell. You'll still smell good down there hours later.

For men

Genital hygiene goes both ways. You won't enjoy sex as much if your husband does not keep himself groomed and smell free down there as well. Push him to keep himself shaved and clean.

Birth Control

This wouldn't be a complete sex manual without addressing birth control. Of course, no method is 100% effective (other than abstinence!) but there is a wide difference in how effective the different methods are.

Pulling out (coitus interruptus)

The easiest (and least effective) contraceptive method is pulling out. It's exactly what it sounds like. You have normal sex but your husband pulls out before ejaculating. It works about 75% of the time, meaning you've still got a good chance of getting pregnant. If you want a surefire way of avoiding pregnancy, this is not it.

Condom

The method that's most commonly thought of when thinking about birth control is the male condom. In addition to birth control, it's a barrier contraceptive so it helps prevent STD transmission (insha'Allah something you'll never have to worry about). The best condoms are effective a little over 80% of the time. That's probably a lot lower than you were expecting! The reason condoms are so common in our society is not because they're extremely effective for birth control but instead because they're very effective in blocking STD transmission. This is a huge problem among non-Muslims who have multiple partners (and their partners have multiple partners) so condoms are strongly emphasized. This is less of a concern for a couple with bilateral monogamy and so condoms are probably not the best choice for birth control if you really want to avoid pregnancy.

How to put a condom on is simple but for those who are completely bewildered, here it is:

Take it out of the package and make sure it's the right way around. Squeeze the end with your index finger and thumb and place it on the tip of his erect penis. Keeping the tip of the condom squeezes, unroll it down the length of his penis. Make sure there's some slack at the place you squeezed so that his cum has a place to go.

Pill

The most common type of pill is a combination of estrogen and progestin. These make your mucus thicker to stop sperm from entering your uterus and also stop ovulation so that your eggs don't leave your ovaries. These are effective 90% of the time for most women. They can also have some side effects like spotting, breast tenderness, headaches, depression, and decreased libido.

Hormonal birth control

These work similar to the pill but aren't taken orally. You can get an implant (Implanon or Nexplanon) and it'll last for 3 years. It works 99.5% of the time.

You can also get "the shot", i.e. Depo-Provera. You have to go get it every three months. It works about 95% of the time but some people experience weight gain with it.

There's also a patch and a vaginal ring that work in a similar manner.

IUD

These seem to be the most popular. Your doctor inserts it into your vagina and it's good for at least 5 years. It is 99.8% effective! A lot of women find that it helps decrease period cramps (or eliminates periods altogether).

Sterilization

This isn't really an option for Muslim women but a tubal ligation will surgically alter your reproductive system so that you can't conceive. Permanent contraception is haram in Islam so this is only an option if a doctor says that childbirth will literally cause you to die.[ii]

Lube

Lube is short for lubricant. Lube is something you use to reduce friction. Basically, it makes it easier for you and your husband's skin to slide against each other to make sex more enjoyable. Different women secrete different amounts of fluids when they're aroused. For some women, even mild arousal can result in enough natural lubrication that they don't need any outside lube. For others, even when they're extremely aroused, their body doesn't secrete a lot of natural lube. If you're in the latter category, it's always a good idea to have a bottle of lube stored near the bed for when you have sex.

There are four types of lubes. Water based, silicone based, hybrid, and oil.

Water based lubes are the most common. Since they're water-based, they're easy to clean, won't stain clothing or sheets, and can be used with condoms without causing them to tear. They can also be used with sex toys.

Silicone is probably the second most common lube. It has a really unique feeling, almost silk-like. It lasts longer than water based lube so you don't have to reapply as often. You can also use silicone with condoms without a problem but they do break down silicone sex toys. In addition to the silky smooth feeling of silicone lubricant, it comes in handy during shower sex. It won't wash away like water lubricant so if you're having shower sex, use it!

Hybrid lubes are kind of in between a water and silicone lube. They feel like water but last as long as silicone and wont' wash off in the shower. If you're planning on using just one lube, start out with this one.

Oil based lube have a number of drawbacks. They break down latex condoms. They're hard to clean up. But, they feel *amazing*. And for some guys, there're few things hotter than seeing their wife with a naked shiny body. If you're using oil-based lube, don't use it for penetrative sex. Use it when giving a sexy massage, a handjob, or breast sex.

Some companies even sell flavored lube. This can make oral sex easier if you or your husband are bothered by the natural smell down there even despite good hygiene.

Before going out and buying an entire bottle of lube that you might not use, start out with a travel sized option. These are usually good for one or two uses and will give you a feel for each one. After trying them, you'll be able to decide which one works best for you.

When having sex, feel free to reapply lube as needed. Lube evaporates so even if you're wet and slippery when you begin, you might feel a little bit dry later on. Just take some lube and rub it over his penis or condom to get things sliding smoothly again.

Final thing to keep in mind is that a lot of lubricants are sperm-unfriendly. If you're just have sex for fun, this doesn't matter. If you're trying to get pregnant, look for a lube that says TTC (trying to conceive) on it. These are formulated to not change pH so that the sperm doesn't die because of the environment.

Kegels

Kegels are a pelvic floor exercise that every woman should do (actually, every man should do them too). Doing these exercises regularly will help you in so many ways. Most doctors recommend it to help with urinary incontinence after pregnancy but it has so many more benefits. It will increase the strength of your orgasm, increase vaginal tightness, and give you the ability to tightly squeeze your husband when he's inside of you.

Think about what muscles you use to hold your urine in when you have to go. Flex those muscles. If you can't figure out which muscles those are, do this. The next time you go the bathroom, you're your urine midstream. You might not be successful at actually stopping the stream but at least you'll know which muscles you need to use. Those are the muscles you'll be exercising with Kegels. As an aside, don't make it a habit to stop urinating midstream though. That increases the risk of a bladder infection.

Once you've figured out which muscles to use, tighten them and hold for five seconds. Then relax for five seconds. Do this four or five times. It's important to keep them relaxed for an equal amount of time! The relaxing is as much a part of the exercise as contracting. Work up to keeping them contracted for 10 seconds and relaxing for 10 seconds.

For best results, focus on isolating and tightening just those muscles. When you start, you might find yourself relying on your butt muscles or abdomen muscles. As you strengthen your pelvic muscles, you'll be able to isolate it to just contracting them and nothing else.

Do at least 3 sets of 10 repetitions a day. You can do it more if you'd like. My Ob/Gyn recommended doing it every single time I'm at a stoplight. There are kegel weights that you can use if you so desire but simply doing the contraction and relaxation without inserting anything will still get you good results.

Sexting

Sexting is a touchy subject. Texting your husband is naturally going to have some sexual overtones at times. Talking dirty to him over text at times is fine (and in this book, I'll teach you how to do it).

The problem comes in when you send explicit pictures to each other. I know many young couples exchange nudes but I would strongly warn you from this. I'm not saying this as someone who's afraid or unaware of technology. In fact, the opposite. There are actual dedicated websites on the internet which post pictures of Muslim women in varying states of undress. Men go onto these websites and arouse themselves by looking at a woman going from full hijab to wearing nothing.

The sad reality is that you simply don't know where your pictures can end up. Divorces happen and angry ex-husbands can be vindictive. Even if your husband is the most honorable man in the world, phones can get lost, misplaced, or even borrowed. It takes just a few minutes to transfer an entire digital library of images to a computer. Once your photos are on someone else's computer, they can be disseminated all over the world in a matter of minutes. As many Hollywood celebrities found to their horror last year, many phones back up their photos to a cloud. That cloud can (and has been) hacked, resulting in thousands of images being leaked over the internet.

I personally know a hijabi sister, very active in her community, who made the mistake of sending such photos to her husband. After her divorce, they were leaked over the internet along with her name. He denies having anything to do with it but the fact remains that whenever a person Googles her name, nude images of her show up in Google. Even after spending money and hiring someone to contact websites to remove her photos, an occasional one will still resurface under her name.

It's really not worth the risk.

With all that said, I'm realistic. I know most couples will *still* at least occasionally send each other nude images. If you're going to do it despite my advice to the contrary, make sure to take these precautions:

1. Don't send a picture via text or other medium where it can be easily stored on his phone. Use Snapchat. There are still plenty of ways to save Snapchat photos but they require intention and effort. In the event of a divorce, your ex-husband won't have a trove of nude photos saved on his phone that can be "accidentally" leaked onto the internet.

2. Don't include your face in such pictures. In the event of those photos finding their way onto the internet, not including your face allows the images to be kept separate from your identity.

3. Never, never, *never* keep nude images stored in any format. The day your little kid swipes through your phone's photos to find an 'Eid picture and stumbles upon photos of you naked is a day that will permanently scar both of you.

Dirty talk

This is not for everyone but some people get *really* turned on by talking dirty. On the other hand, some people get *really* turned off by it. This is where communication comes into play. Talk to your husband beforehand. I firmly believe that in a happy sexual relationship, the other person should indulge the predilections of their spouse even if they're not turned on by it, so hopefully if you're into it and your husband is not, he'll at least give it a try. One last thing. Dirty talk does not HAVE to involve profanity. It can, and the profanity turns a lot of people on, but if you and your husband don't feel comfortable with It, you can still dirty talk without profanity.

First and foremost, keep context in mind! Dirty talk is when you're feeling lusty. It is *not* something to introduce when you two are in a cuddly, romantic move. If your husband kisses you on the forehead, look you in the eyes, and then says "I love you", do NOT respond with "I love you too. Now drill my pussy with your rock hard dick." Just no. Talk dirty when you and your husband are in a carefree mood, having fun, maybe flirting. not when he's telling you that you're the love of his life.

Another thing to keep in mind about context is how your voice sounds. If you're out in a parking taking a nighttime stroll, it would make sense to take a breathy voice and whisper into this ear "I can't wait for you to fuck me when we get home". Saying that same thing in a high-pitched squealy voice won't have the desired effect. On the flipside, if you two are already in bed together, it *would* make sense to squeal "Fuck me harder baby". Using a sultry whisper voice here doesn't make sense.

Point here being: dirty talk is not just knowing the words but also the context. Know when to use it and what tone to use.

Another thing about dirty talk: communication is also non-verbal! In addition to your tone and context, use the rest of your feminine wiles. Sure, you can whisper to him "Baby I want you inside of me" and get a rise out of him. OR, you can lean in, place a hand on his chest, breath your hot breath on his ear and say in a soft tone "Baby….I…want….you…inside….of….me."

Ok, so you've decided you want to at least try some dirty talk. What exactly do you say? Well, if you're not having sex at the moment, you tell him what you want to do with him. If you are having sex at the moment, you tell him what you're liking about it. It's really that simple.

Here are a few examples to use.

If you're really shy, you can start out with a simple text. Here are some tame starters:

"Looking forward to you coming home today. I have a feeling we're going to have some fun!"

"When you get home, don't be surprised if I'm not wearing clothes"

"I can't focus at work! I keep thinking about your body and what I want to do with it"

"What do you want me to wear tonight?"

Things to say when you're outside home and you want to build up the sexual tension

"I wish I was home so I could do the dirty things to you that I want to"

"I want to rip your clothes off right now."

"You know, if we were at home, I'd probably have your dick inside my mouth right now"

"You look so sexy in that shirt"

"Walk in front of me so I can check out your butt"

When you get started talking dirty for real, here are few beginning sentences:

"Mmm, baby, that feels soooo good."

"I am SO wet right now"

"I could spend all day between your legs"

"I'm getting close"

"Is that a bulge I'm seeing in your pants?"

Kick it up a notch:

"I love riding you like this"

"I love sucking your dick so much"

"You have such a hot ass"

"It's so hot when you pin me down like this"

(If you're being dominant)

"Get down on your knees and service my pussy"

"You cock belongs to me"

"Shut your mouth and get naked. I'm gonna have my way with you and you can't do anything to stop me"

(If you're being submissive)

"I've been a bad girl who needs spanking"

"Pull my hair and Make me your bitch"

"I want you to handcuff me and fuck me any way you want

"Fuck me like I'm your personal slut"

Flirting with other men

This should be a no-brainer, but women who get their marital advice from pop-magazines and pseudo-psychology sources may have heard the popular refrain that "flirting with others is actually healthy for a relationship". No, no, no! If your husband has even a shred of gheerah, this is only going to distance him from you and possibly even lead to divorce.

Never, ever play get-even games by flirting or letting men give you attention. You'll find this tip in superficial girlie magazines. It might even work for some women in the short term, getting their husband to pay attention to them out of jealousy. In the long term, it breaks down the relationship. If the only way you can hold a relationship together is by manipulating your husband with these tricks, you need to see a marriage counselor to determine whether the marriage is worth staying in.

Part II

First time

Many of you will be reading this right before marriage. Those of you aren't, feel free to skip to the next section.

The mixture of emotions you're feeling right now is unique. Nervous, excited, worries, anxious, scared, eager, afraid. All tied together as one!

Some couples start with sex on their wedding night. Others delay it. There's really no right or wrong when it comes to this. If you feel comfortable enough with your husband, you might decide to dive in headfirst. Many women, however, find it better to delay it until they're comfortable with their husband. Personally, I would recommend not having penis in vagina intercourse on your first day. It would be better to get comfortable with kissing, handjobs, getting fingered, and oral sex before moving on to vaginal penetration. By the time you actually have penetrative sex, you and your husband will already be very comfortable with each other's bodies.

Pain

Contrary to popular belief, sex should not be extremely painful, even when you lose your virginity. Yes, it might not be as comfortable as it will be later on, but excruciating pain? That shouldn't happen. If it is too painful the first time, have him pull out. Perhaps you need more foreplay, perhaps you should add more more lube, perhaps you're not mentally ready, or perhaps you have a medical condition. Don't force yourself into it if the pain is unbearable. That pain is telling you that something is wrong.

Bleeding

Not every woman bleeds her first time. The more relaxed you are, the more you've played around with your husband, and the more lubricant you use, the less the chance of bleeding.

Think about how nervous you are. Your husband is just that nervous too, maybe more. Remember, one of the best ways to torpedo your relationship is to make fun of your husband in bed or make him feel insecure (if your husband does either of these to you purposefully, see a marriage counselor immediately). The first time (or two or three or five), many guys find themselves unable to sustain (or even achieve) an erection. This doesn't mean his body doesn't find yours attractive! It's a physiological response to nervousness. Once he gets to the stage where he can achieve erection, don't be surprised if the first couple of times he lasts only for a few seconds. Be encouraging but at the same time, don't stop once he ejaculates. You can still have fun in bed when he's not hard! Have him go down on you or finger you if the sex wasn't enjoyable. This is another reason why I recommend not starting off with PIV sex. If it doesn't go 100% well (which it never does), at least he has some experience in how to pleasure you properly.

Communication

Tell your husband he needs to be gentle the first time. This seems like a no-brainer but if his view of sex has been warped by porn, he might think all sex is fast and rough. There'll be time for hard and rough sex later but the first time, slow and gentle is the way to go.

Start with foreplay until you're wet. Have him insert at least two fingers inside of you before moving on to his penis. Once you're relaxed and comfortable, guide him inside. It should NOT require a lot of force. If you can't get it in, pull out, go back to foreplay, and focus on him fingering you. Then try again. If it still won't go in, see a doctor.

If he keeps popping out, don't worry, happens. He'll learn with time how much he needs to thrust.

If you don't orgasm through penetration, you're in the majority. You enjoy kissing your husband, right? Does that end with orgasm? Probably not (if it does, please send me tips on what he does so I can tell my husband). Enjoy sex for itself. Think about orgasms and penetrative sex as different. You can have one without the other or you can have both. Worrying about orgasmings during sex diminishes your pleasure. You'll be focusing on what's not happening rather than enjoying what is. Relax, enjoy the pleasure. We'll talk about increasing the chance of orgasm through penetrative sex but enjoy sex with or without orgasm. After he's climaxed, guide his hand down your clitoris to bring you to orgasm. Sex is NOT over when he's satisfied. It's over when both of you are.

Kissing

I know, I know. You might be rolling your eyes saying to yourself, "I thought this was a book about sex. Why waste my time talking about simple stuff like kissing?" That's the wrong way to think! Don't dismiss the sensuality of a great kiss. Physical intimacy is more than just penis in vagina. It's a complete package and often begins with a kiss. The very first intimate physical act you'll likely have with your husband is kissing. Don't overlook it!

More than just the *first* intimate act you'll have with your husband, kissing is actually one of the *most* intimate acts a couple can do. Think about all the senses which are centered in your face. Your sight, your smell, your hearing, your taste. It's no wonder that couples who divorce often stop kissing long before they stop having sex. Sex can be romantic and intimate but it can also be simply passionate and lustful. Kissing, however, always conveys love. In the hookup culture we live in today, many people will have casual sex with others while refusing to give them a kiss. There's a natural tendency to equate kissing with love.

As you read the following tips, realize that a lot of this will flow naturally between you and your husband. Don't get too caught up with details. Especially your first time, just go with the flow. As you and your husband become more familiar with each other, you can start incorporating some of the techniques I mention.

Before even beginning to talk about *how* to kiss, I have to make sure to talk about oral hygiene. This is a real issue! You don't want your husband to not kiss you because your breath smells bad! Same goes with the reverse. If your husband's breath isn't the greatest, find ways to subtly nudge him in the right direction. Schedule a dentist appointment for him if you need to. Make sure you're brushing twice a day. Floss your teeth regularly. Get a non-alcoholic mouthwash and use it daily as well. If bad breath is still a problem, see a dentist! Finally, although not really *hygiene*, use chap stick to keep your lips soft. All of this will enhance the kissing experience.

Start by making eye contact with your husband. Give him a small smile and a light touch before beginning the actual kiss. Maybe put your hand on his face or touch his leg. Make him anticipate the kiss.

Begin slowly and gently. You don't want to rush into the kiss and bump teeth. Start with a kiss on the lips. Tilt your head to the side so that you don't bump noses. When your lips meet, slowly squeeze his lips into yours.

After a while, you can morph this into a French kiss. Do this by slowly opening your mouth wider until you can put your tongue into his mouth and touch his tongue. Use your tongue. Tease him with light flicks. Go back and forth into each other's mouths. Trace the edge of his lips with the tip of your tongue. Explore his mouth! Feel his gums and teeth with your tongue. Make sure to give him opportunity to reciprocate.

Don't just kiss on the lips. He has other kissable parts too! Work on his neck and collarbone. Bite, but gently. Nibble his earlobe or neck. Maybe his bottom lip. If you're adventurous, give him a hickey. Kiss his neck with a slightly open mouth. Suck in the skin. This will leave a mark so be careful where you do it!

Remember, a kiss is more than just your mouth. Use your hands. Don't leave your hands limp in front of you or on your lap. Explore your husband's body. Put your arms around his neck. Touch his arms. Run your hands down his back or chest. Run your fingers through his hair and massage his scalp. His body is exclusively yours for the rest of your marriage! Explore the goods!

Tease him in the middle sometimes. Pull back for a second or two and look him straight in the eyes. Wait for him to pull you back in. Time then when you need a break for air so it doesn't break the mood.

Whisper in his ear. "You are so hot." "I've been waiting all day to kiss you". Exhale your warm breath onto his ear. This drives men crazy.

If you want to take some control when kissing, put your hand on his chin. You can manipulate his face from side to side and control where you kiss him.

Mix things up. You don't have to do all the above every time. Try one or two, mix things together.

While this is about mouth to mouth kissing, remember, he has an entire body to explore. The lower back, the butt, and the stomach are sensitive areas that are fun to kiss (and be kissed at!).

After it's done, tell him how fun it was! Marriage is not a time to be stoic. Let him know you enjoyed it. "That was amazing!" "I can't get enough of kissing you!". If he did something that you especially liked, let him know so he does it more often! Communicate!

Hand jobs

Ok, so moving up from kissing is the hand job. Like it sounds, this is when you work your magic on his penis using your hand. Some couples never try this, figuring it's a boring middle-ground between kissing and sex. Don't be fooled, a good handjob can be incredibly pleasurable for your husband.

You might be tempted to morph a handjob into oral sex as things heat up. It's a natural progression to go from hand on his penis to mouth on his penis. I'm not saying *never* go from a handjob to oral sex **but**, don't always do that. At least try a few straight handjobs to completion with no oral involved and see how much pleasure you can elicit from just a handjob.

The great thing about handjobs is that you don't need much set up. You don't need to be in the bedroom (but do need privacy of course!), don't need a mood, and you don't even have to worry about any smell from hours of sweating! If you have lube handy, it can make the handjob feel even better but it's certainly not a requirement.

In theory, a handjob is simple. Wrap your fingers around his penis and move your first up and down with slow, measured strokes. But this isn't a book about simple sex, it's a book about how to have "mind-blowing" sex. So here are some tips to move your handjobs from basic to amazing.

Even though a handjob is often seen as foreplay (even though you absolutely can make it the main act), it gets even hotter when you do some foreplay *for* the handjob. Start with a kiss and while he's focusing on that, move a hand down towards his pants. With your husband's pants on and still zipped, start by rubbing over them. Instead of starting right over his penis, I'd recommend putting a hand on a thigh and working inwards. Draw little circles with your index fingers, spiraling in to his penis. When you get over it, massage it a little bit and feel his hardening erection. Use your index finger to scratch over his balls and penis. If you get just the right angle, it'll drive him crazy.

After a minute or two of this, unzip his pants and tug down. Pull down his underwear as well. Once you release his penis (hopefully erect by now!), gently graze it with your fingers. Move from top to bottom. He might have a few drops of precum at the tip. Don't waste it! Using one finger, spread the precum over the tip of his penis.

Grab his penis and begin stroking it up and down. Ask him how firm he likes it. Some men enjoy a firm grip while others prefer something more gentle. Regardless, you don't have to be as gentle with his penis as you do with his testicles. It can take much more pressure than his testicles. Start out slow and gradually increase your speed. The fast you go, the shorter he will last, so keep that in mind. Keep your wrists constantly in motion.

Maintain eye contact. It's easy, especially as you've been married longer, to go on autopilot and give him a handjob while you're watching TV or reading a book. While this is fine in moderation, you don't want it to appear that you've got more important things to do and are only grudgingly giving him some sexual pleasure that doesn't interfere with your own schedule.

While stroking him, there's a few things you can do to vary the sensations and increase the pleasure. Don't try all the different techniques at once. Introduce one or two each time you give your husband a handjob and see which ones he enjoys the most. Mix them up to keep things fresh.

Techniques

Instead of using your full hand so your palm is stroking him, switch to using just your finger tips. The feeling of five or ten little points of contact instead of one big one will give him a unique sensation.

 Use both hands, one over the other, if his penis is long enough and/or your palms are small enough. Even if your hands are big or his penis is shorter, you can still use two hands by making an "o" with the thumb and index finger of one hand and the palm of the other. Once he's completely erect, you can occasionally throw in a twisting movement as you go up and down.

The glans of his penis is the most sensitive part. If it's too sensitive for him, only use light touch. If it's not try this technique to mix things up. Move your thumb to the tip of his penis instead of wrapping it around with the rest of your fingers (kind of like holding a computer joystick). Use the thumb to tease around the head while you stroke up and down normally. Other places that are more sensitive are the ridge where the head meets the shaft (corona) and the ride that runs straight along the underside of his penis (frenulum).

You can use one palm to completely envelop the top of his penis while continuing to stroke with the other.

You can try stroking him just upwards, one hand after the other, and then just downwards. Switch up your grip and change from a full grasp to using just a ring formed with your thumb and index finger Experiment and play around! You don't have to try all of these during one session!

Don't forget his balls. Men *love* it when their balls are paid attention to. These can be very sensitive though so be careful. Try massaging and stroking them. Hold them in your palm and gently roll them around. Do NOT hit them or squeeze them—it can be very painful.

Vary your positions. You can give a handjob side by side, sitting between his legs while he's lying down, kneeling between his feet as he sits on a sofa/bed/chair. Hug him from behind and then grasp his penis underneath from between his legs.

Be prepared for ejaculation! Tell him to tell you when he's about to cum. Depending on whether you're dressed or not, either let him blow into your hands or over your face, neck, breasts, etc. If you don't want any of that, pull up his underwear and let him ejaculate there.

And yes, sometimes (maybe most times), a handjob will only be a prelude to sex. In that case, have him stop you before he ejaculates so that you save it for the sex. As always, make sure you're giving him feedback and communicating during the handjob. "Mmmmm, your cock feels so warm and nice in my hand", etc. See the chapter on talking dirty if you need tips.

Blowjob

This is one of the most important sections of the book. There are few things which will make your husband lust after you more than the sight of you on your knees in front of him, giving him oral sex.

Blowjobs are something where your skills can continuously improve. Even with no experience, your first time giving him a blowjob will be an event to remember. After that, it can only get better as you get more adept at various maneuvers. You'll find that oral sex is very versatile and can be done in so many positions and so many places.

Before you give a blowjob though, make sure that your husband is shaved down there. Go back and review the section on genital hygiene. You want your husband to be clean and (relatively) odor-free down there. Hair does not make oral sex appealing.

Start your blowjob by kissing him like normal Think about it as a prelude to the main act. While you're kissing him, use one hand to slowly beginning rubbing his crotch. Once you feel his penis hardening, unbutton and unzip his pants, pulling them all the way down.

Now that his penis is exposed, get down on your knees. The submissive nature of this position makes it arousing for a lot of people. During the times you prefer something less submissive, have him lay down on a bed and then position yourself between his crotch. It's still an inherently submissive act, but this slightly decreases that aspect of it.

Don't start by immediately taking his penis into your mouth. Work outwards and come in, building up the anticipation. Kiss around his crotch and groin. Tickle his balls with the tips of your fingers. Spend some time coming closer to the penis, enjoying the sexual tension that builds up as you tease him below.

When you decide to begin, start by gently stroking his penis with your hand. Again, you're building up the tension as he anticipates your mouth meeting his penis. Do this for just 30-45 seconds. Then, lower your mouth and take his penis in. Keep your lips wrapped around it and move it in and out. The more saliva you can get, the better it'll feel for him. Use your tongue to massage his penis while it's moving in and out. As you get more comfortable, take more and more of him inside of you with each stroke. There's a good chance you'll eventually take him so far in that you trigger your gag reflex. Don't worry, it's natural.

The most sensitive part of a penis is called the frenulum. This is right where the head of his penis meets his shaft, on the back portion of his penis. Gently flick this while sucking him to stimulate it. Some men don't have a frenulum, depending on the method by which they were circumcised. It's not a big deal if it's not there.

Now, you don't *always* have to build up the tension like this. Some days, you may feel like cutting straight to the chase. Simply undo his pants, take his penis out, take it in your mouth, and begin pleasuring him. The key to a spicy sex life is variation. Don't always do one or the other. Some days, you'll prefer the slow, anticipation building blowjob. Other days, you'll prefer to go straight to the main event. Keep it fresh by switching then up.

With the basics out of the way, there are other things you can do in a blowjob to make it interesting. Don't use all these techniques at once. Think about them like spices on food. You add one or two per dish, not all. So the first time, have a completely plain blowjob, just your mouth and up and down. Add in one technique next time, then another the time after that.

Techniques

Kiss! It's not just for the mouth! Yes, kiss his penis. You can do small quick pecks or long wet sloppy kisses. Not only is it erotic and arousing to watch for him, it'll give your jaw a rest from having him in your mouth.

Make eye contact. Seeing his penis inside your mouth while you're looking up at him will really turn on your husband. Don't be shy, he enjoys seeing you like this, so indulge him.

Talk during the blowjob. You might wonder how you can talk if your mouth is otherwise occupied. Well, during a blowjob, you don't have to have his penis in your mouth the entire time. Make use of your hands intermittently to give your jaw a rest. That's when you talk to him. Tell him how much you're enjoying giving him a blowjob. Ask him how he likes the feeling. Talk dirty to him if you're comfortable with that.

A small variation is to apply pressure with just your lips. Take your husband's penis into your mouth and make an O shape with your lips. Press down using just your lips. Then, bob your head up and down, taking his penis in and out of your mouth.

Do not, do not, do NOT use your teeth on a blowjob. This is a tip found in many women's sex magazines and you have to wonder if it's a revenge plot from an estranged ex-lover. Imagine if your husband was using his teeth when performing oral sex on you. Don't do it.

Licking. A blowjob isn't just taking his penis into your mouth. Use your tongue in its entirety. Treat his penis like a lollipop and use your tongue to lick it from the base to the very tip. Spend more time at the head, working your tongue all around and under it to stimulate his nerves. Your tongue is surprisingly muscular and you can really work his penis using just your tongue. Spiral your tongue around the top of his penis. Move it in circles and alternate directions and speed.

Just like in a handjob (which you can be doing alongside a blowjob), don't forget about his balls. They're fun to play with and pleasurable for him. You can lick them, kiss them, or suck on them. You can switch to stroking his penis with your hand while you take his balls into your mouth and then reverse it, fondling his balls with your hand while you take his penis into your mouth. Just don't neglect them.

Use your hands! In addition to working his penis with your hands when you take a break to rest your jaw, use your hands *while* in the process of giving oral sex. You're probably going to have at least a few inches of his penis hanging out of your mouth. Use a hand on the exposed shaft to give sensation there as well.

Suck him. This requires energy but is very pleasurable. Wrap your lips around his penis and take the first few inches into your mouth. Suck on it gently. This will cause your cheeks to grab his penis and make him moan.

Cheek sex. A lot of women want to deep throat their husband (next section) but simply can't do it. This is an easier alternative that mimics most of that feeling. Clamp your mouth shut and then take his penis into your mouth, pushing it against the outside of your check. His penis will be between your teeth and your cheek. Now suck in, trapping his penis inside that pocket. It creates a unique feeling, very similar to that of deep throating.

When you're giving oral sex, make sure you tell him to communicate when he's about to ejaculate. There's a difference of opinion, but most scholars say swallowing is haram.[iii] You can finish by having him cum on your face (facial), onto your chest (pearl necklace) or just collect it in your hand. If you don't mind changing the sheets, you can just aim his penis away from you and have him ejaculate on the bed.

Deep throat

Deep throating is when you take your husbands penis all the way into your throat. It's not just a blowjob with your mouth, you literally take it into your throat. Some men and women enjoy it, others despise it. The biggest issue with deep throating is gagging. About a third of women don't have any gag reflex. If so, deep throating is much easier. If you do have a gag reflex, deep throating is much harder. Once you get it under control, however, it becomes relatively easy.

You can look online for tips on how to desensitize your gag reflex and get it under control. Instead of going through all of that trouble, however, it's often much easier to use a throat numbing spray to temporarily desensitize the gag reflex. You can find these on Amazon for less than $10.

Especially early on, don't deep throat your husband without telling him. It requires practice and gentleness on his part to make it work without being painful. So make sure he knows exactly what you're doing before you do it. Tell your husband what you're going to attempt before trying it. You want him to be as still as possible the first few times you try.

Positioning is important for deep throat. Do this on a bed. Lay flat on your back with your head hanging over the edge. Have your husband stand or kneel so that his penis is at the level of your mouth. This opens up your throat and makes the angle easier for deep throat. Have him go in slowly and tap the bed with your hand when you want him to back out.

Remember, you have to breathe as well! Try breathing through your nose. Depending on the size of your throat and his penis, even this might be impossible. If so, you'll have to take breaks every 10-15 seconds to breathe. There's just no way around it.

Many women simply can't deep throat or never enjoy it. If that's you, don't worry. There's plenty of other fun things to do in the bedroom.

Massage

A sensual massage is one of the hottest things you can do. It can be either be done on its own, or before or after sex (as foreplay or as post-sex enjoyment). Like a kiss, massages are a unique way of conveying love, not lust. A good massage doesn't have to last long and doesn't require much preparation.

If you're doing it on its own or as foreplay, it's good to set the mood. Have the right ambience for a sexy massage. Dim the lights, burn some bukhoor, maybe set some soft music in the background (if you follow the fiqh position that music is fine). A good trick is to take one of your colored hijabs and drape it over a lamp shade to give off a colored glow. It can really change the ambience of the room.

Pick a product to massage into him. Coconut oil is the standard but there are special warming oils and flavored massage oils (if you want to use tongue) that you can consider.

A good massage is slow and sensuous. Remember, this involves the whole body from the top down. Don't jump straight to his penis!

Start at the very top, at his head. Yes, massage that too! Rub your fingertips in small circles over his scalp. The feeling of ten individual points of contact going in all sorts of directions is amazing. Apply as much pressure as you want, there's no chance of you hurting his scalp with just the pressure of your fingers.

One place which feels *very* good to massage is the pressure point right in the middle of the forehead (the place where cartoon cyclops have their third eye). Take both thumbs and apply pressure there for a minute. It does wonders to relieve the tension. While you're doing this, massage the sides of his forehead as well. Keep your thumbs pressed in the middle of the forehead and use your other fingers to massage his temples.

Then massage his facial bones. Trace the angle of his jaw with your fingers and apply pressure on his cheekbones and you walk your fingers over his face.

Move down to his neck and shoulders. The neck is an often overlooked erogenous zone. Feel for the indentations in his neck and apply pressure there. Rub the tense muscles on the side of his neck before moving down to his upper back. When you get to his shoulders, use your full hands on each shoulder to push down on his muscles. You can even use your elbows to apply more pressure if he enjoys that. Remember, use lighter pressure on the skin over the bones here and more pressure on the skin overlaying the muscles between bones.

Work your way downwards, spending about 10-15 minute on each section. Take each arm and massage down from the shoulder to the end. Use your knucles to kneed his palms. Massage his fingers by twisting each of them in a closed fist.

Massage his butt, pressing in with your thumbs. Get the back of his thighs, and push in hard. As you move down to his thighs and legs, you'll find that they're more muscular and you have to push in harder. Move outward along his inner thigh, massaging all the way. If he's comfortable, try and push in to his perineum, the area between his scrotum and his anus. Work your way all the way down, rubbing to his feet, his heels, and his ankles. If he works a job that requires a lot of standing or walking, this will feel *so* amazingly good.

Don't forget the other side of his body! The clavicle, the chest, the breast bone, the nipples, all of them also feel good to be massaged!

As you're massaging him up and down, vary the pressure that you're applying. Pay attention to his responses. A soft moan means you're doing great. A harsh intake of breath means you're going too hard. Some men like that, though, so if you hear it, ask him if he wants you to apply less pressure.

Now that you've gone top to bottom, move back up to his penis and testicles. Give him a handjob but make it slow and sensual. Don't do it with the goal of making him ejaculate. Use slow, long strokes with the palm of your hand. Use lots of oil to keep it wet. Massage his testicles too but very gently.

Depending on what the mood is, you can finish the massage by turning up the intensity of the handjob until he ejaculates or just finishing without any orgasm. A sensual massage is a treat by itself!

Unlike other acts, this is one where less talking is actually sexier. If you need to say something, use a soft, sultry voice. A sensual massage is all about non verbal communication.

Stripping

Before I even begin, stripteases are not for everyone. Some women and their husbands will find it exhilarating. Others will try to suppress their laughter when performing/viewing it. If stripping is more comedic than sexy for you or your husband, don't waste time trying to force yourselves to enjoy it. It's just not for everyone—and that's fine!

The best place to strip is your bedroom, provided you have enough space. The bed is right there and you two have already started associating the room with naughty time. If it's not large enough, the living room will have to do. If you're doing it in the living room and have kids, **absolutely** make sure there is no way they can come in the house at that time. This is reserved for a time when all the kids are at school or otherwise firmly separated from the building.

Choosing what you wear when you strip is key. You have to plan so that you have multiple layers of clothing on, with sexy clothing at the end. Nylons and garters are uniquely alluring. If you're going with this, wear your panties *over* the garter belt instead of under. This allows your husband to pull off your panties while leaving the garters and stockings intact, making it look more enticing when he gets to that part. Over this, wear a skirt that's easy to take off. For your top, make sure you have a sleek bra and then choose something like a blazer on top. Saris are a super sexy outfit to wear when stripping. Some women might feel awkward doing this, but I'd recommend to keep adding layers until you're presentable enough to go outside. Meaning wearing a hijab or even a niqab. Going from fully covered, pious Muslimah to ravaging him in bed is part of the turn on in a striptease.

Once you have your outfit prepared (or before), set the mood by lighting bukhoor or other incense. Like a massage, striptease is a sensual action so you need the proper setting.

Remember, in a striptease, *you* are taking control. This is one where you're dominant. When he comes home from work, grab him by the wrist and take him to where you're going to strip for him. Push him, —firmly— where he should sit. Give him a soft kiss and then walk away.

As you walk away, make sure it's slow and seductive. Put some movement into your hips as you do so. When you get as far as you intend to, stop. Look over your shoulder while still facing away, and take the outermost layer of your top off.

Take a step back towards your husband. Put your hands on either side of your hips and lower your skirt/pants to the floor. Bend forward while you're doing this so that your butt is front and center for your husband.

Each striptease will be different depending on what you're wearing. Your instinct might be to take your hijab off first. Switch it up though. Your husband might find the sight of you in a hijab and nothing else to be very sexy.

When you're undoing your bra, again, do it slowly. Face the other way. Slip each shoulder strap down before undoing the bra from behind. Throw the bra at him over your shoulder. At this point, all he sees is your bare back. *Then* turn around and let him get a view of your breasts.

A really good move to do to turn him on is to come up to him and sit down while straddling one of his thighs. Move up and down his thigh. Take it all the way to his knee and then grind your crotch into his knee.

If you have the time, try doing a practice run by yourself before doing it with him. Even then, you might find that the first few times is awkward. That's fine, you have a lifetime to perfect it! Like I said, for some couples, this isn't a turn on at all. If that's you, that's fine! There're other ways to spice up your sex life.

Positions

So, now to the real meat of the book. Sex positions. This is the best way to vary your sex life. Some couples never move beyond missionary position. If that's what you two enjoy, that's perfectly fine! However, not every couple wants to stay vanilla every time. In the following pages, I'm going to talk about 100 different positions for you and your husband to try. You'll find that you're drawn to

Girl on top positions

These are for when you're feeling a bit more dominant and want to take control.

Cowgirl

Cowgirl is the most common position when the woman is on top.

Have your husband lay down on his back and straddle him. Put your legs on either side of his waist such that your knees are on the bed. Now you're in control. Take his penis with your hands and guide it inside of you. Depending on the length of his penis and the depth of your vagina, it might be painful to sit straight down. This is a position where smaller penis length is preferable. If he's hitting your cervix and making it uncomfortable, lean forward and angle yourself so that it's more comfortable. You can put your hands on his chest, on the bed, or on your thighs. Then start riding him. The first time you do this, you'll likely find yourself bouncing up and down on his penis. Later on, you can cary this by moving your body back and forth, basically grinding against his pubic bone. This is fantastic for stimulating your clitoris and the rest of your vagina. As you get even more comfortable with this position, you can combine and grind against his pubic bone *while* bouncing up and down. Use your hips. Move them around. Back and forth, up and down, side to side, even some swirling. Instead of thinking about it as his penis being inside of you and then you moving around, think about it as you stroking his penis with your vagina. The bulk of the motion should be originating from your hip area. Full body bouncing is nice for his viewing pleasure but it's the hip motion that is really going to work his penis.

Remember, you're in control here. You can change the angle of entry by shifting back and forth. Your husband doesn't have to do anything in this position and the first few times you try it, it's better for him to just lay back and enjoy the view. He'll love seeing your breasts bounce up and down as you ride him. As you two get used to each other, he can start contributing by using his hips as well. A simple up and down thrusting movement can add some variation. He can also gyrate his hips in a swirling motion to stimulate your vaginal walls during this position. Depending on how you two feel about anal play, he can also insert a finger or two into your rectum or, at the very least, push you up and down while holding your butt.

Lying cowgirl

This is a small variation of the cowgirl position. Have your husband lie on his back and the edge of the bed. His feed can be touching the floor or just hanging along the side of the bed. Straddle him with one leg on each side of his body and your pelvis meeting his. Then lean forward and bring your boobs into contact with his chest. He trades the chance to get a view of you riding him with the feeling of your skin against his. The pelvis-pelvis contact can give you some clitoral stimulation if you throw in the right hip action.

Asian Cowgirl

This is a small variation of the cowgirl position. Instead of straddling your husband, you squat over him. Start out by getting in the regular cowgirl position. Lean forward, put your hands on either side of his body to steady yourself, then rock back into the squatting position (yes, the position you use in toilets back home). Women with thicker thighs find that this position gives them greater range of motion. It also requires you to have very strong thighs and lower body muscles. Even women who are athletic and in great shape can't keep this position for more than a minute or two.

Reverse Cowgirl

This is very similar to the cowgirl position, but with you facing the other way. Your husband lays down on his back and you straddle him with your knees on either side of his thighs. You're facing away from his face, giving him a view of your back, not your breasts. If you have a larger butt, this is a good position to allow him to play with your butt while you're having sex. Don't be surprised if he delivers some light spanks while you're riding him in this position. Some women find the reverse cowgirl to be an easier position to start out with than the cowgirl position. The lack of eye to eye contact takes some of the anxiety and nervousness out of the equation.

Reverse Asian Cowgirl

Combine the previous two

Lunge

If you've ever done a lunge, you'll know from the name that this position also requires a good deal of strength and flexibility. This is really just a small variation of Asian cowgirl. Once you get into position, you keep your front foot planted but your rear leg extended out behind you and between your husband's legs. In a sense, you're doing a "lunge" while positioning your vagina over his penis.

Amazon

This is one of the most difficult to perform women-on top positions. It requires flexibility for both partners and an above average penis length for the male. It's also one of the most dominating positions for the woman so it's worth trying at least once. For this position, your husband should lie down on his back like he would for any other woman-on-top position. Then, he should bring his legs up and bend his knees. You squat down on him while he's pulling his legs close to his chest. Then you just squat up and down to allow him to penetrate you. As you do this position, you'll find that he automatically pushes you back upwards with his thighs. You might find that leaning against his thighs helps take the pressure off your legs a bit.

Be careful in this position. Go slow so that you don't accidentally hurt his penis.

Kneeling Amazon

This is a variant of the Amazon. To make it a little bit easier on the legs but still requires an above average amount of physical stamina. Get into the same position as Amazon but on your knees instead of squatting. You can stay in this position longer and also have more flexibility in choosing your angle. With this position, you have a chance to enjoy some deep penetration.

Reverse Amazon

Another variant of the Amazon. You get into the same position but face away from him rather than towards him. The difference in angle can give you a very unique sensation.

Kneeling reverse Amazon

Combine the previous two

Inverted Missionary

This is exactly what it sounds like. It's like missionary, but inverted. Your husband lays down with his legs together. You straddle him with your knees on the bed, facing him. Learn forward so that you're resting on him. You can be as active as you want in this position, using your hips to move up and down his penis. Or, you can have him be the active one and do some thrusting. This is a good position to try because it flips the usual position. Hopefully, being a "limp fish" isn't a problem for you after reading this book, but if you were one, this position would let you know how it feels for your husband when he's in missionary and you're being a "limp fish". You can always spice up this position by kissing him and holding him close for more skin to skin contact. If you want to play up the dominant angle, grab his arms and pin them over his head. To add some clitoral stimulation, pretend you're doing a crunch and move your crotch up towards your body while in this position.

Sybian

Have your husband lay down on an ottoman (or a soft-cushioned stool or something similar). Straddle him like your'e in the cowgirl position but since you're not on a bed, you'll have your feet planted on the ground. You can use your legs to bounce up and down him. You can also grind on him or thrust forwards and back. Remember, leaning front or back can help change the angle of entry. Your hands can either go on his stomach or stimulate your clitoris to increase the chance of an orgasm. This is one that requires a lot of energy to do with not as much of an increase in pleasure.

Thigh master

For this position, your husband should start out by lying on his back. He should extend one leg and bend the other at the knee, planting his foot on the bed. You should mount him by facing away and straddling his raised thigh. Basically, have one knee on either side of his leg and lower yourself onto his penis. Hold on to his leg but use your own legs to help you bounce on him. One of the great things about this position is that you can directly rub your clitoris onto his thigh. In a way, you're humping his thigh while you're doing this.

Worm

Have your husband lay on his back on the bed with his legs spread as much as possible. You sit on top of him while facing away Then you lean forward and slide your feet toward's his head, kind of like a pushup position. Do this very slowly and stop if it's uncomfortable for him. This position puts your butt front and center and gives your husband a great view. In addition, he can see his penis coming in and out of your vagina, which is a major plus.

Doggy style positions

These positions are more submissive for you and allow your husband to be dominant. While these make for very intense sex, they're not very intimate.

Doggy style

The name gives away how you need to position yourself. Get down on all fours with your legs spread apart. Your husband will get down on his knees and enter you from behind. There's not much that you need to do in this position. You can simply stay on all fours while he thrusts into you. If you want deeper and harder penetration, push back into your husband with each stroke. To change the angle he's coming in at, change the arch of your back. You can increase and add more arch by sticking your butt as far out as possible or decrease and make the arch less. If you can support yourself on three limbs, you can use one hand to reach down and rub your clitoris yourself in this position.

This is a very primal and submissive position. This is not a position for when you want to make *love* but instead, a position when you want to get *pounded.* Since this is a very submissive position, you might find that it's a good position for your husband to spank you in. He can grab you by the waist or shoulders to manhandle you a bit more in this position. If you're feeling very submissive, have him tie your hands behind your back. He'll be in complete control.

Standing doggy style

This is doggy style but with both of you standing. Find a secure object to hold on to and bend over. You can keep your legs together or spread them apart to adjust your height. It's a good position for where you don't want to (or can't) lay down. Sex in the kitchen, in the bathroom in front of the mirror, etc.

Bendover position

This is almost exactly like standing doggy style but with you bending over at your waist. You need to be very flexible for this so some women simply can't do it. For those that can, however, place your hands on the floor to balance yourself. The visual is amazing for your husband, letting him see your back and hips and butt. It allows for very deep penetration for you, making for intense sex. This is a good position to try in the shower.

Basset Hound

Get down on all fours like normal doggy style. After that, however, lower yourself even further towards the ground. Spread your knees out and push your butt backwards to lower your waist. Get onto your elbows and spread them out so your breasts are close to the ground. This allows for very deep penetration. If your husband has a shorter penis, this might be very pleasurable. If his penis is longer, this might be a little bit painful (unless you like his penis hitting your cervix).

Bulldog

Again, position yourself on all fours like normal doggy style. This time, however, bring both of your legs together. Your husband should place his feet outside of your legs so he can enter you in a slight squatting position. The tighter you keep your legs together, the larger your husband will feel to you.

Fire hydrant

This position requires some flexibility. You begin in the standard doggy style position. His knees should be inside yours. Then, your husband will lift up one of his legs and plant his foot on the floor to your side. The end result will be that your thigh is resting on top of his thigh, making you look like a dog urinating on a fire hydrant (hence the name!). This position lends itself well to very deep thrusting and possibly g-spot stimulation.

Frog leap

This position doesn't start out like the rest of the positions in the doggy style family. Squat down frog style, with your knees bent and leaning forward on your arms to stay balanced. Your husband gets behind you on his knees and enter in just like normal doggy style.

Leapfrog

Not to be confused with frog leap. You begin by getting into regular doggy style position. Instead of propping yourself up on your knees, however, rest your chest and head on the bed. Push your butt high upinto the air. Your husband will enter in with his legs close together inside of you. If you do this in front of a wall, you can place your hands and push back with a good bit of force into your husband. This will make each thrust stronger and harder. This position makes for very deep penetration. This may be a positive or negative depending on the length of your husband's penis and the amount of depth from your vaginal opening to your cervix.

Prison guard

This is even more dominating than the previous positions. Begin by facing the same direction as your husband. Bend over so that you're looking down at the floor. You can spread your legs to change your height as needed. Put your arms parallel with your body. Your husband holds on to you by your wrists and thrusts in. You're the prisoner, your husband is having his way with you. This is a position to wait to try until you and your husband are comfortable with rough intercourse. He should know what amount of rough is pleasurable and what amount is painful for you before you two try this position. You can mix this up by getting on your knees or laying prone instead of both standing.

Stairway to heaven

This is doggy style when you have a home with carpeted stairs. Make sure there's no one in the house before doing this, of course. Put your knees on a lower step and your hands on a higher one. Your height is going to determine how many steps should be between your knees and your hands. Your husband will stand on the step below your knees and then enter into you.

Final furlong

Doggy style positions in general are more lustful and less intimate. This is one of the more intimate and sensual of the doggy style positions. It also requires the right furniture. Finding the right furniture to do this on is half the battle. Find a decent sized footrest or ottoman that can seat both of you. Sit down, straddling the footrest, and leave slightly forward. Basically, the footrest is your saddle and you're a jockey in a horse race (hence the name, final furlong). Your husband sits behind you and enters in. This doesn't require as much effort as the rest of the doggy style positions, making it good for slow, intimate intercourse. You can lean backwards again him and pt]ut your arms gently around his head or back to make it more intimate.

Turtle

This is an extremely submissive position. Get into position by resting on your knees. Lower yourself down until your butt is sitting on top of the back of your ankles. Lean as far forward as you can. Grab your legs to help lean further forward. Husband enters from behind and thrusts in. You'll find that you're almost immobile in this position, making it great for when you want to be dominated.

Pump

Start by positioning yourself on a sofa with your legs bent slightly. Your husband will penetrate you from behind while standing. You can put your arms in front of you onto the

This is a position where you're submissive. This is mostly your husband thrusting in and out. He's in a good position to reach around and rub your clitoris in this position.

Face to face positions

Delight

This is an intimate position. Sit at the very edge of your bed (or any surface that's 1-2 feet above the ground). Open your legs wide. Your husband should kneel on the floor between your legs. He enters from there and thrusts in. Depending on your heights, you may need to use pillows to fix your alignment. You can put pillows underneath yourself or under your husband's knees. Angles are also important. When you first try out this position, experiment with angles. You can do any angle from sitting up straight with your arms around his neck to leaning so far back you're almost laying down. With time, you'll find which angle is most pleasurable. Keep in mind though that the further back you lean, the more you increase the distance and the less intimate this position becomes. Don't be afraid to use your own hands for some clitoral stimulation in this position.

Dancer

This requires flexibility and strength. Start off by standing upright and facing your husband. Lift one of your legs so that your husband can hold it at his side. If you're flexible enough, you can wrap it around his waist. Once your leg is wrapped around him (or held at his side), he can enter you and start thrusting. He should have one hand around your waist and the other holding your leg with his arm. This is a very intimate position and allows you to hold him close while you're having sex. You can wrap your hands around his waist to make it more intimate, or even put then under his arms and grab him by the shoulders. If you get tired, you can switch the leg that you're standing on. Most women will find that they can't hold this position for more than a minute or two.

Slow dance

Quite similar to the previous position. You both stand up facing each other. If your husband is taller than you, he'll have to bend his knees so that he can position himself well to enter you. Open up your legs a little bit to make it easier for him to do so. Then you just wrap your arms around each other and make gentle thrusts while hugging. This is already very intimate to begin with but you can make it even more so by using your hips and legs to maximize skin on skin contact. If height difference allows, move your hands up to his head and massage his scalp with your fingers.

Spooning (non doggy style rear)

Bodyguard

For this position, you both need to stand up and facing the same direction. Your husband will enter you from behind. If there's a substantial height difference, he'll need to bend his knees to enter inside of you. After that, it can be a slow, intimate case of him thrusting or you pushing back. It's up to you which of you two does the work. If he wants to do it, he can thrust in and out. If you want to do it, you bush yourself in and out. You can wrap your arms behind you, around his hips and butt to pull him in. Or, have your husband wrap his arms around you and hold you closer to make it more intimate.

Teaspoon

Your husband gets on his knees and opens up his legs relatively wide. You then get on your knees in front of him while also facing the same direction. You keep you rknees together and he can enter you from behind, wrapping his arms around you. He can wrap them around your waist, hips, or breasts. This is an intimate position, so he should be thrusting gently. This isn't a position for hard, passionate thrusts. Either your husband or yourself can play with your clit to increase pleasure in this position.

Lying on your stomach

Irish Garden

Your husband needs to first sit down on your bed with his back straight and upright. His legs should be out in front of him and opened up wide. If he isn't very flexible, he can bend his knees to make it more comfortable for him. Get down on all fours facing the same direction as him and lower yourself onto his penis. Straighten out your legs, one on each side of his waist, and then lower yoru head and shoulders onto the bed until you're laying on your stomach. In this position, you'll be doing most of the work. You can use your hips to move up and down in a rocking motion. Your husband can't really thrust here, but instead, he can put his hands on your butt or waist and rock you.

Jockey

Lay face down on your bed with your legs straight and together. Your husband straddles you with his knees on either side of your waist. After he enters, he leans forward just like a jockey riding a racehorse. This is a *very* passive position. You basically lie there and let him have his way. At most, you can raise up your butt a bit in sync with his thrusts to make them a little bit harder. You can simultaneously grind against a pillow while in this position to increase the chance of an orgasm.

Rear entry

This is very similar to the previous position. You lay down on your bed with your legs straight and together. Your husband gets on top of you but instead of straddling you like in Jockey position, he does it with his legs togethers, just like in missionary position. The rest is the same.

On your back position

This includes the famous missionary position, the one position that is used most often in sex. Your husband is more dominant in these positions.

Missionary

This is the most common sex position, period. You might find that it's your go-to position. It works for almost everyone regardless of fitness level, flexibility, and weight. Don't worry, you're not "vanilla" just because you enjoy this position (not that there's anything wrong with being vanilla if it satisfies you two in the bedroom).

You lay down on your back with your legs open. Your husband gets on top with his legs between you. He can rest some of his weight on his elbows to avoid crushing you. On the other hand, you might find that you like the feeling of him allowing some of his weight to push you down onto the bed. Experiment to see what is most pleasurable.

To increase pleasure in this position, have him grind on you while he's thrusts. Basically, he needs to move his pelvis up and down while thrusting so that his pubic bone pushes into your clitoris. Don't think, however, that just because he's dominant in this position that you should do nothing. That's a recipe for the dreaded "limp fish" syndrome. Be vocal, don't be shy in letting out any moans of pleasure. Use your arms to wrap around his neck or head, or even to grab his back so that you can pull yourself up to cause even deeper penetration. If you're into BDSM, he can lightly choke you with one or two hands while in this position. Read the section on BDSM and safe words before trying that though.

What to say during sex

Probably the most common complaint men have when they're not satisfied with sex is "she's like a limp fish". A lot of women *want* to show their husband they're enjoying sex but don't know how to express that.

Interestingly, the key to not being a "limp fish" in bed begins outside the bedroom. Let him know you're thinking of him or that you're looking forward to the night. This lets him know that he's not the only one getting pleasure out of sex.

Once you two are in the bedroom and his clothes start coming off, run your fingers and hands over his body. If you like something about his appearance or his smell, compliment him! Men don't get compliments but love them just as much as we do. When was the last time a friend complimented you on your outfit or on your hair or on anything? Probably recently. Ask your husband the last time a friend complimented him on anything. There's a good chance he won't be able to think of any example. So compliment him, he'll feel so great!

Give him verbal feedback during sex. If he's doing something right tell him how good it makes you feel. You don't have to be detailed. It could be something as simple as "Right there" or "keep going" or "more" or "don't stop". If he's doing something wrong, give him guidance! Some women are shy about this but it's very important. If he doesn't know what he's doing wrong, how can he improve it?

Ask him how *he* feels? It can be something as simple as, "Do you like that?" or "Does that feel nice?". He'll give you feedback and you can continue or adjust accordingly. A grunt or moan is a positive feedback

How to be a freak in bed

Be open to trying things.

That includes what's in this book as well as things your husbands suggest that aren't in here. *However,* you have to draw the line at what is haram. If your husband wants you to do something that is clearly haram, don't give in. If he is pressuring you or manipulating you into doing those things, it's very important to consider whether this is a marriage worth staying in. I know two women who were pressured into anal sex with their husband. They both acquiesced. Not too long after that, they were divorced, citing the abusive nature of their husband. Trying new things in bed should be a healthy and mutually enjoyable part of your relationship.

Enjoy sex

Don't think of this book as simply a way to please your husband in bed. It's a way to please yourself as well! If you focus only on doing things your husband wants, you're going to feel like you're faking or simply providing a service to him. You want to enjoy sex for yourself too. Don't get caught in the false narrative

Don't leave it up to him to spice things up

Don't be shy of voicing your preferences. Just like you're open to trying new things, your husband should be open to them too. Some days do what he prefers, other days do what you prefer. Hopefully there's a large overlap between what you two prefer!

Be confident

Your husband is not doing you a favor by having sex with you. He wants it just as much as you do (maybe even more). Maybe you think you're overweight or your boobs aren't big enough or your legs are toned enough. Take a deep breath. Your husband wants you. He married you and (assuming you married for deen and he's pious), you're the only woman he's going to be having sex with. Men are just as worried as we are. They worry their penis isn't long enough or thick enough or they won't last very long or they're last too long or they're not muscular enough. The difference is that men want sex so bad, they push that aside and move forward. Take that same attitude!

Variety

Routine is the enemy of a good sex life. Switch things up. Try different positions, switch between being dominant and submissive, explore things you haven't done in the past. Don't fall into the rut of only missionary sex.

Initiate

This goes back to being confident. Remember how I said men are just as worried about their bodies as we are, they just want it so bad that they push it aside? Well, when you don't initiate, he'll start wondering what's wrong with him. He'll think you're not interested or don't' find him attractive. He won't voice it, most guys are too stoic to say it, but it'll really strain your relationship. You don't have to initiate every single time but if you can get it to 50/50, that would be perfect.

Dressing sexy in the bedroom

This section is about dressing up *at home.* When you're outside, you should be dressed modestly and in a manner that doesn't draw attention to your beauty. Inside the home, however, is a different story.

The most important part to dressing sex is to find out what your husband think is sexy! Not all men are the same. Some men enjoy seeing their wives in thongs. Others find the sight of plain white panties to be intensely arousing. If you want to dress sexy for your husband, you need to know what he finds sexy.

At the same time, you should also find what makes *you* feel sexy. If it's the same, great! If not, alternate outfits between what makes you feel sexy and what your husband thinks is sexy. If a certain outfit makes *you* feel sexier, it'll shine through and translate into more enjoyable sex. So dressing up isn't simply a visual treat for your husband, it can be enjoyable for you as well (both in the dressing up part and for what happens after the clothes come off).

The trick about dressing sexy is to *not* reveal too much. He's seen your body. He knows what you look like naked. The key to a good sexy outfit is as much about what you hide as it is about what you reveal. Knee length boots and a mini skirt will expose only your thighs but can drive him crazy with desire.

To know what he finds sexy, *ask.* Especially early on in the marriage, he might be hesitant in suggesting what you wear, afraid that he might offend you or make you feel insecure. So you'll have to be direct. "What color of lingerie do you think I look sexy in?"

An easy way to start getting sexy outfits is to pick a weekend to go shopping. Put it all on him. He gets to pick out anything he wants for you to wear and you agree to wear it. You might be surprised to find what he thinks you look sexy in. Pay attention to his responses after you buy these clothes. Which ones prompt more compliments? Which ones lead to more aggressive (or more sensual) sex when you wear them?

Keep a variety of sexy outfits for the bedroom. While lingerie can quickly get very expensive, you can start with something simple that still arouses him. Buy an inexpensive pair of short shorts and a tight tanktop. You might find that this is his favorite outfit for you to wear. Or maybe a sports bra and leggings. Wear low cut dresses or pair a long top with no pants. All those outfits that women wear to clubs and bars? Well, you get to wear them at home for your husband!

Lingerie is sexy and you'll definitely want to buy some. Like I said though, it can get expensive and it's not the only way to dress sexy. Over time, you can gradually build a collection. If you can, try to buy one outfit a year, maybe for Eid.

Fantasy roleplay goes hand in hand with dressing up. A plaid skirt and button down shirt with a tie to play a schoolgirl or a nurses outfit or a secretary's outfit. Your imagination is the key.

Finally, there are specific exotic outfits you can purchase. It may be too extreme for more vanilla couples but if you or your husband find dressing up to be arousing, it's something to consider. Whether it's a latex catsuit, corsets, body harness, body stockings, etc, there's plenty of very exotic sexy clothing you can bring into the bedroom.

Dry humping

There's a unique sexual tension to dry humping. The friction of your clothes against your labia and clitoris is extremely stimulating. It's also something that you can do with your husband when you're on your period.

You can initiate this very easily. When just kissing, just start rubbing up against your husband and let it go from there. Alternatively, you can take him completely by surprise and press your body into his when he's doing something mundane like watching TV on the couch.

One of the best body parts to dry hump while he's sitting is his knee. Straddle his thigh and rub your crotch into his kneecap. Other good body parts to grind against are his butt and the heel of his hand.

If you're in bed, the cowgirl position is best. Straddle him and grind against him until you're panting.

Touch, touch, touch! It doesn't matter if you have clothes you, the feeling of a hand on your body is arousing. Be handsy with him and have him be handsy with you.

If you're venturing into BDSM, dry humping works very well with bondage and you being dominant. Tie him up so he can't move and then slowly grind against him. The tease will drive him crazy.

Breast sex

Men love playing with boobs. Can you blame them? Sometimes women forget how awesome boobs are because they're always with us 24/7. If you don't believe how awesome they are, surprise your husband one day by greeting him topless one day. You'll see where his eyes are trained.

Playing with boobs is great by itself. If you want to kick it up a notch though, there's boob sex. This is great for when you're on your period and still want to have sex. It's also great for when you're not on your period. It's just great.

Start with regular foreplay. This is a time when you want lots and lots of lube so have it ready. The wetter, the better. If you know you're not going to be using condoms, coconut oil makes an excellent lube for this. In addition to the actual lubrication, shiny boobs will arouse your husband even more.

Once you two have gotten into the foreplay, rub his penis over your breasts. Then, cup your hands on either side of your breasts and push it inwards, trapping his penis in between. Interlace your fingers to trap them together. You've made the equivalent of a vagina for him to thrust in.

Don't worry if his penis slips out. This happens all the time. You'll find it happening less and less frequently as you practice but it never completely stops.

There are a number of positions you can use. There are three main ones. Him on top, you on top, and you on your knees. For him on top, lay down on your back with your husband straddling you over your abdomen. If he's long enough, you might be able to flick your tongue out to lick him on the upstrokes. For you on top, have him lay on his back and you lay on your front between his legs. Last position is with him sitting down on the bed with you on your knees between his legs. Depending on the size of your breasts, some (or all) of these positions might not be possible. If so, don't worry, there are other ways to have fun!

Pearl Necklace

This is when your husband ejaculates on or around your neck. Yes it's messy but for some women, there's an enjoyment in being sexually marked (and for men, enjoyment in sexually marking you). Be sure to close your eyes. If he ejaculates hard, that pearl necklace can turn into a facial and it can sting if his cum enters into your eye

Femoral sex

This is kind of a "oh duh" thing once you think about it. This is mostly for when you're on your period and are still feeling frisky. You press your thighs together and your husband puts his penis between your thighs. I'd highly recommend lube if you don't want your husband's penis to get sore.

Quickie

"Quickie sex" refers to sex that lasts a very short amount of time. Think less than 5 minutes from beginning to end. You both might actually not even completely take off your clothes during it!

This is not a romantic type of sex session. This is more of an expression of lust and unbridled sexual tension. Both types of sex are necessary for a healthy relationship.

As Muslims, the greatest obstacle to a quickie is the fact that you have to know that you can take a ghusl before the next prayer time ends. This makes it a lot harder to have an afternoon quickie in your husband's office behind closed doors. There are still times you can make it work, however. For example, in the morning! After Fajr and before he leaves for work is a great time. If he's asleep and ahs morning wood, wake him up with a blowjob. When he's awake, climb up and ride him.

Shower sex

It's Sunnah so you have to at least try it.

If you wear makeup, remove it before getting in the shower. You don't want mascara streaming down your face while trying to look seductive!

The best part about shower sex isn't the actual sex, it's the intimacy and foreplay. The water isn't just a backdrop! Have your husband wash you and vice versa. Lather up and clean every inch of his body. Alternate between using your palms and using a loofah. Feel every nook and cranny of his body. Alternate who's under the water! This is intimate in and of itself. Sometimes, all you want after a hard day is showering together, no actual sex in the shower. Make sure to use a silicone or hybrid lube because the water is going to rinse away all the natural lubrication.

If you do have sex, before you let him enter you, make sure you rinse all the soap off of both of you. You don't want the soap coming into your vagina and causing an infection!

Shower sex is fun but it can be dangerous. This isn't the time to try contorted positions. You want to be firmly grounded when you actually have sex. You can be pushed against the wall (or pushing him against the wall), bent over and holding on to something, or sit on the floor. If you two really enjoy in, consider investing in a suction cup handle to give help support yourself in the shower.

Because the shower really cleans everything up, this is a great time to give or receive oral sex.

Rough Sex

Before I begin saying anything, let me give you a disclaimer: rough sex is not for everyone. You may not be into it or your husband may not be into it. There's nothing wrong if you don't like it. There's plenty of other ways to enjoy a healthy sex life without rough sex.

Rough sex shouldn't be the only type of sex you have. There are certainly days when you want to be ravaged and treated like a piece of meat by your husband. But that should be balanced with gentle, romantic lovemaking. Even if you really enjoy rough sex, intersperse it with more sensual sessions as well.

What if *you* want to be dominant?

Take the lead. Grab him by the hand and lead him to your bed. Or, push him onto the bed and start unbuttoning his shirt. Even the most rough and masculine guys will be turned on by their wife taking the lead. Try and be assertive. Be the one who turns foreplay into sex. Push him onto his back, straddle him, and take control. If you've never done it before, you'll be astonished by how much it turns him on.

Things you can do to rough sex up:

Grab his hair. To pull hair correctly, push your nails up the back of your husband's neck and into his scalp. Grab his hair from his roots. This is very important and makes a distinction between pleasure and too much pain. Grab the roots, not anywhere else. Your nails should be grazing into his scalp while you do this.

Scratching and biting. Digging your nails into your partner's back and holding them tightly lets them know how turned on you are. Don't worry, your husband can take the pain.

Being immobilized is also a great feeling. Have your husband pin your arms down and not let be able to move as he has sex with you. Turn it the other way at times and attempt to immobilize *him* as you have sex with him. This might require some suspension of disbelief since he probably *is* able to move even if you pin him down. But the fantasy is part of the fun!

Make sure to have lube handy so that you don't have any vaginal bleeding due to microtears from him thrusting too hard.

Maybe you want your husband to be rougher and he's not getting the hint. Communication is key here. Tell him what you like, "I get so wet when you grab my hair in bed." Or "I orgasm so hard when you throw me down and take control"

Rough sex goes together with dirty talk. Some women really find it arousing to have a specific term they use to refer to their husband when having rough sex. Some go with "Sir" others with "daddy" or others with something they've come up with. Find something that turns you on and use it. Some women find it arousing to be objectified by name when having rough sex. For example, being called a whore or a slut or a bitch. Finding that you're aroused by these when having sex does *not* mean that you have some hidden inferiority complex or you're less of a feminist. Being called names like this when enacting a fantasy with your husband who loves and respects you does not mean you think these words are appropriate to be used by men towards other women.

Forced sex fantasies

"Rape" fantasies are extremely common for women. You're not weird for wanting it. It has nothing to do with an actual desire to be raped or a sign of mental illness. There's a push to relabel "rape" fantasies as "forced sex" fantasies because that's what they really are. It has nothing to do with wanting to go through the trauma of rape. Instead, it's a fantasy of being ravished and taken forcefully. There's something arousing about that.

With that said, this is not for everyone. For men *or* women. Some women want nothing to do with forced sex fantasies. Some men want nothing to do with forced sex fantasies. This is one place where I make an exception to the rule that we should accommodate our spouses's fantasies and predilections. If either of you is disturbed by this, don't even try to attempt it.

Communication is *so* important if you go ahead with this. You must establish a safe word that both of you can use. You also have to establish what the boundaries are of what can be done in terms of physical aggression. You have to agree beforehand if you'll be using any instruments like handcuffs or gags.

See the next section on BDSM for some more help in terms of forced sex fantasies.

BDSM

BDSM stands for
Bondage/Discipline/Dominance/Submission/Sadomasochism. The
acronym isn't really important. 50 Shades of Grey has brought it into the
mainstream but many healthy couples were partaking of it before the
book gained notoriety. By the way, 50 Shades of Grey is to BDSM what
pornography is to sex. If your knowledge of BDSM comes from 50 Shades
of Grey, it's wrong. That book is a great explanation on how NOT to do
BDSM.

Before we talk about BDSM, some basic terminology.

Top is the one who gives sensation

Bottom is the one who receives sensation

Dominant refers to the person who has the power (or takes it).

Submissive refers to the one who doesn't have the power or who gives it
up.

Switch is one who switches between roles.

Sadist is one who enjoys giving pain

Masochist is one who enjoys receiving pain.

These are just terms. In real life, you don't pick one and play that role.
You'll probably mix and match. Usually, the husband will take the
dominant role and the wife the submissive role but switch it up.

Be careful when navigating BDSM. Some of this can be straight up haram
(drinking urine??? Cutting the other person???).

BDSM should only be done if you absolutely trust your husband. This is
not something to try out the first time you have sex. It is not something to
try with a husband who is physically or emotionally abusive. You need to
be 100% comfortable with your husband before venturing into BDSM
territory.

Safe words are big in BDSM. This should be something other than "stop"
or "no" because those words might be part of your roleplay where you're

just pretending to struggle against him. A good safe word to use is red/yellow/green. Think about it like traffic lights. Red means you need to stop. Yellow means you don't need to stop but he should slow down. Green is to assure him to keep going. If you're gagged, you should have some alternative to a stop word. This could be holding something in your hand that you drop to indicate you want to stop.

Start slow when you begin exploring BDSM. Very slow. Begin by just trying one thing and just that one. Then add in another. Don't try too much at once. For example, let's say you want to try getting blindfolded and getting whipped. Don't try both together at first. Pick one. Let him spank you with a whip one time. Then, the next time, add in the blindfold. It might not seem like much but BDSM can quickly get overwhelming so take things slowly.

Bondage

In short, bondage is limiting someone's movement with restraints. You can do this with almost anything. Rope, leather cuffs, chain, bondage tape, even your hijab. Always have EMT shears around if you're doing bondage.

Bondage is when you tie each other up. Lightweight cuffs are the best for beginners. Fuzzy looking handcuffs look comfortable but leather or neoprene are actually more comfortable. Blindfolds also fall under bondage as well as gags. Silicone ball gags are the best ones to start out with. These are smaller and often labeled as "beginners".

If you've never been tied up, try it. It's a paradoxically liberating form of sex. You totally give up control and allow your husband to pleasure you.

Make sure that restraints aren't too tight. You should also avoid using things which can tighten if you struggle. Some people use scarves and ties but this can potentially tighten and cut off circulation. The safest option is to use actual restraints created for sex.

Discipline

Discipline refers to both physical and mental discipline. Among these are spanking (either with a hand or a paddle), flogging, denying the other person access to their own body or yours, and playful biting.

Spanking.

 Spanking is probably the most common BDSM fantasy that women have. Spanking usually goes hand in hand with talking dirty. Ask your husband if you've been a naughty little girl. Whatever his response, say that you need to be punished and that you deserve a hard spanking. When you're getting spanked (or doing the spanking), aim for fleshy areas. The butt and the backs of your thighs are good ones. Be careful of hitting the back because you can damage kidneys there.

There are a number of positions you can take for spanking. You can have your husband bend you over his knee. You can lay spread out on your stomach. Or you can get down on all fours. He can also incorporate spanking into having sex with you doggy style. To really get comfortable, put a pillow under your stomach. He should be aiming for the fleshiest part of your butt, the area where the cheek meets the thigh. If he wears a wedding band, make sure it's off his fingers when he spanks you! After a few spanks, he should caress and massage the area he just hit.

Spanking can actually be quite varied. He can spank you with an open palm or by cupping his hand. He can use a paddle (probably not when you first begin), a whip or riding crop, a flogger, or a cane. If you want to really mix it up, consider wearing Ben Wa balls during the spanking session.

Just like with any BDSM activity, have a safe word. Again, don't use something like "stop" or "ouch" because those are words you might want to mix in for effect. The red/yellow/green technique for safe words works great here.

After finishing a spanking session, apply some cream or balm to sooth your sore butt! If it's too sore, consider asking your husband to tone down the strength or length of it next time. Of course, if you don't enjoy it at all, you don't have to try it more than once.

Spanking doesn't always have to have you on the receiving end. If you want to experiment with being dominant, switch it up and you do the spanking. Some men (and women) feel uncomfortable with that. If you don't like the idea of your husband taking the submissive role in bed occasionally, then that's fine. However, many women find that they enjoy switching it up and being dominant in bed. It's definitely something to try, especially if you're the more submissive type in real life. A lot of people find that their personality in bed is the exact opposite of their personality in real life.

Public sex

Public sex is a common fantasy. Unfortunately, this is going to be next to impossible to do. The one time you can do it is if you can rent a private property. If you can rent a farm in a rural location that has wide acreage or a private island, you might have a chance. If you can snag one of these, having sex under the open air is breathtaking and an unforgettable experience.

Anal play

Having anal sex is haram. Extremely haram.

"If anyone [resorts to a diviner and believes in what he says (according) to the version of Musa) or] has intercourse with his wife (according to the agreed version) when she is menstruating, or has intercourse with his wife through her anus, he has nothing to do with what has been sent down to Muhammad." — Narrated by Abu Hurairah, Book of Divination and Omens, Sunan Abu Dawood, 3895.

"Allah is not shy to tell you the truth: do not have intercourse with your wives in the anus."—Narrated by Ahmad, 5/213

"On the day of resurrection, Allah will not look at a man who had intercourse with his wife in her anus"—Narrated by Ibn Abi Shayba, 3/529; narrated and classed as sahih by Sunan al-Tirmidhi, 1165

"[Make love to your wife] from the front or the back, but avoid the anus and intercourse during menstruation" — Reported by Ahmad and Sunan al-Tirmidhi

"He who has intercourse with his wife through her anus is accursed"— Narrated by Abu Hurairah, Book of Marriage, Sunan Abu Dawood 2157

"If you find someone doing the deed of the people of Lot, then execute the doer and the one to whom it was done." reported by Ibn Abbas, Book of Legal Punishments, Sunan al-Tirmidhi, Book 17, Hadith 40 [Number 1456], classed as hasan.

"Verily, what I fear most for my nation is the deed of the people of Lot." Narrated by Jabir, Book of Legal Punishments, Sunan al-Tirmidhi, Number 1374, classed as hasan

Scholar differ on whether this applies only to anal sex or even to things like sticking fingers there. I would recommend playing it safe and not inserting anything into the anus. There are simply too many things which are perfectly halal to risk doing something so strongly condemned.

Threesomes

I wouldn't even have included this except when looking at online forums, I found several Muslims asking this. It should come as no surprise to you that no, you can't have a threesome. Even if you are in a polygamous marriage and your husband has a co-wive, he can't have sex with both of you at once. You still have awrahs in front of each other.

The simple things

This book is a sex manual but it wouldn't be complete by not reminding you…..pleasure and intimacy is more than just what we've talked about so far. There is real pleasure in just looking at your husband, smiling at his antics, or just holding him close to you, enveloped in his arms.

May you have a blessed and peaceful marriage.

Ameen.

[i] http://seekershub.org/ans-blog/2015/10/14/is-it-permissible-to-have-someone-else-wax-your-body-shafii/

[ii] http://www.drhatemalhaj.com/qa/index.php/2011/03/27/husband-wants-tubal-ligation/

[iii]

http://www.islamweb.net/emainpage/index.php?page=showfatwa&Option=Fatwald&Id=89730

Printed in Great Britain
by Amazon